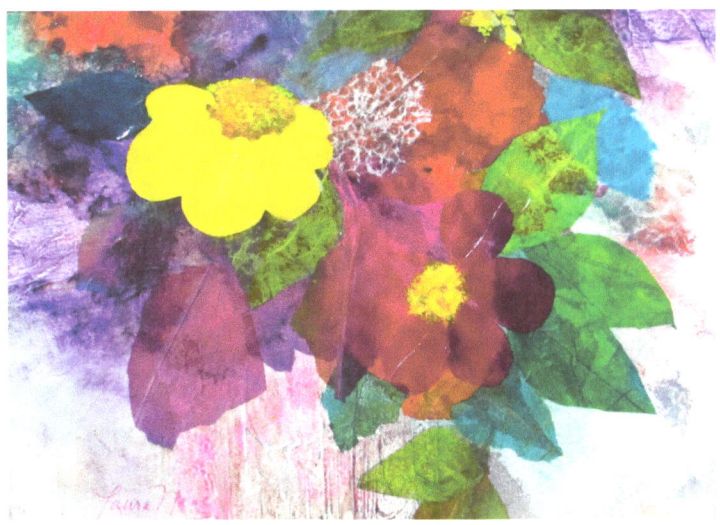

"Flowery" Paper Collage by Laura Nance

Collage Workshop Handbook
Volume 1
by
Laura Nance

Edited by Robert Nance

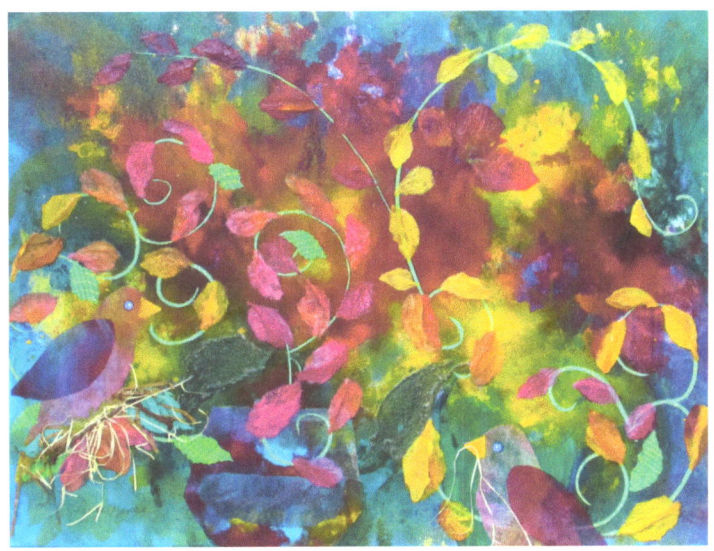

"Villa Bougainvillea" Mixed Media Collage by Laura Nance

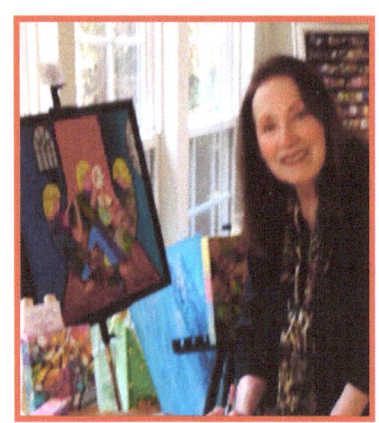

Laura Nance in her Studio

"My desire is to let my paintings reflect the joy and sweetness of a beautiful piece of music... My use of color and light, at times evoking a dreamy world of enchantment and pleasant whimsy, plays in the artwork, as do melody, harmony and rhythm in song. I have an extensive background in the performing arts. I studied and worked as an actress in New York and performed around the world as a professional singer. As an actress, it is exciting to dig deep into the soul of the character to be portrayed. As a singer, I love getting into the very heart of the lyrics of a song. As a visual artist, I am motivated by the prospect of distilling and applying the "joie de vivre" of a live performance to the visual arts. I'm truly amazed and blessed each time I watch the heart and soul of a painting come to life."
- Laura Nance artist statement -

TABLE OF CONTENTS:

An artist communicates from within...

"The artistic vehicle , medium or form of presentation may differ, but one thing is constant - art is a dialog between you and someone else. As an artist you are a communicator. To communicate you have to know what you want to convey, what you want your work to accomplish." Laura Nance

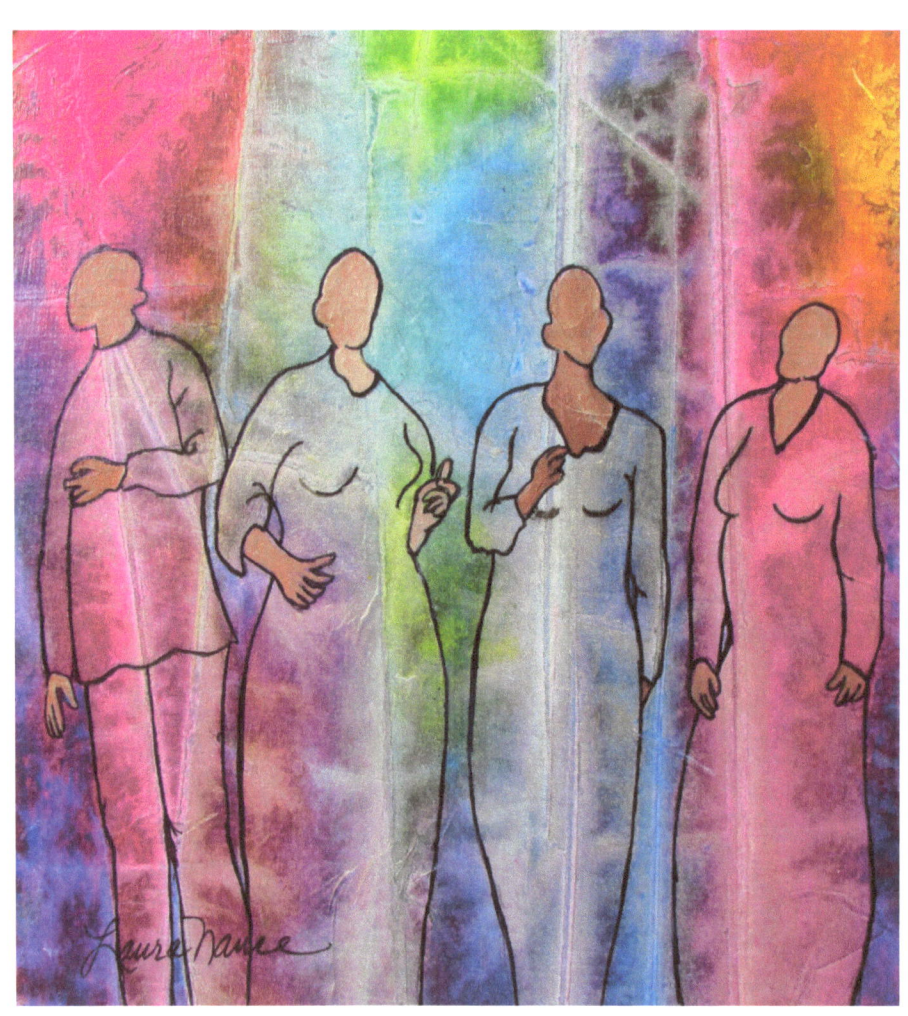

"Hallelujah!" Acrylic and Ink by Laura Nance

INTRODUCTION:
Why would an artist want to collage?

"Why would an artist want to collage? Why add another element to a work that is already so expressive, so complete... so beautiful? Why bother? I'll be honest with you... I would never have thought that I'd be interested in incorporating any form of collage, in my work. However, as I continue to develop my pieces, I am becoming more aware that there are seemingly endless possibilities related to collaging that I have yet to explore... and I find it to be a very stimulating, challenging and gratifying method for creating artwork."

"An extremely accomplished artist from Florida, who paints primarily with oils, was visiting a mutual friend. This friend has a painting by the aforementioned artist and it is one of the most beautiful pieces I have ever seen. I marveled, when the artist saw some of my textured, collage work, and she excitedly expressed how wonderful she thought it was and told me that she wanted to study with me! I laughed... and I said, '...My goodness, you are such a great artist!' And she replied, '...But, I don't know how you do what you do... I want to learn something new from you!"

"...What an interesting experience that was for me... I realized why this woman is as amazing as she is... first of all... such an example of humility... and she is open to new ideas... different methods... wants to keep up with what is going on... while continuing to utilize the great talent she has.
Since that exchange, other artists, of varied skill levels, have requested to take classes or workshops with me to explore both collage and mixed media techniques."

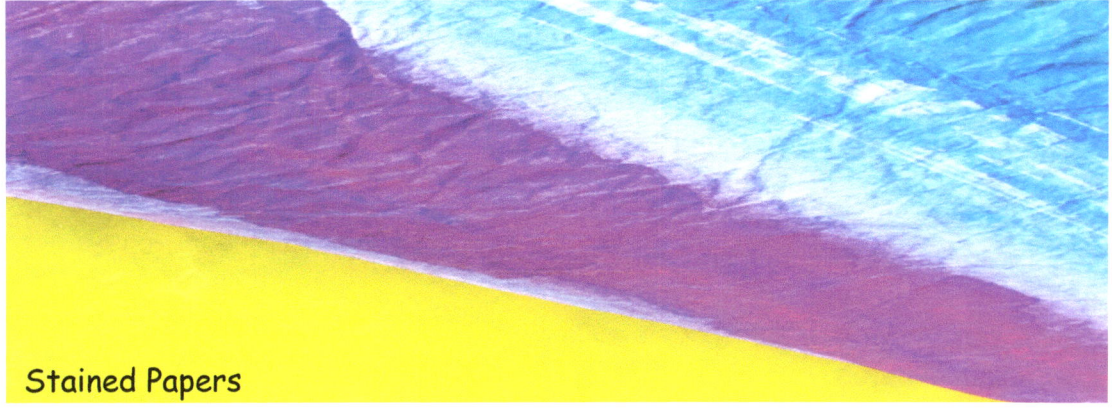

Stained Papers

"We need to keep our artistic talents alive... we need to keep painting, studying, creating! Experiencing that joy... as we continue moving forward... using the gifts God has given us. We need to keep our hearts and minds open... as we embrace that desire to be creative to the very best of our ability!"

Laura

Collage can be simple or complex. The earliest paper collages are thought to have been made by twelfth-century Japanese calligraphers, who used paper and fabric to create backgrounds for their brushstrokes of poetry.
We know that artists in medieval times enhanced religious images using jewels, fibers and precious metals... and so it went on and on throughout the centuries...

I was excited to read that art historians ascribe the first fine art collage to Pablo Picasso, who, in 1912 glued some decorative oilcloth to a cubist still life. Henri Matisse was also well known for his vivid collages of cut and bonded papers. In fact, many of his collage designs have been reproduced as murals and stained glass windows.

Collage offers something for everyone... regardless of skill level. It can be simple for the beginner and intriguing to the accomplished artist.
Carefully selected collage material can add a sense of mystery, excitement or even a glimpse of revelation to your artwork.

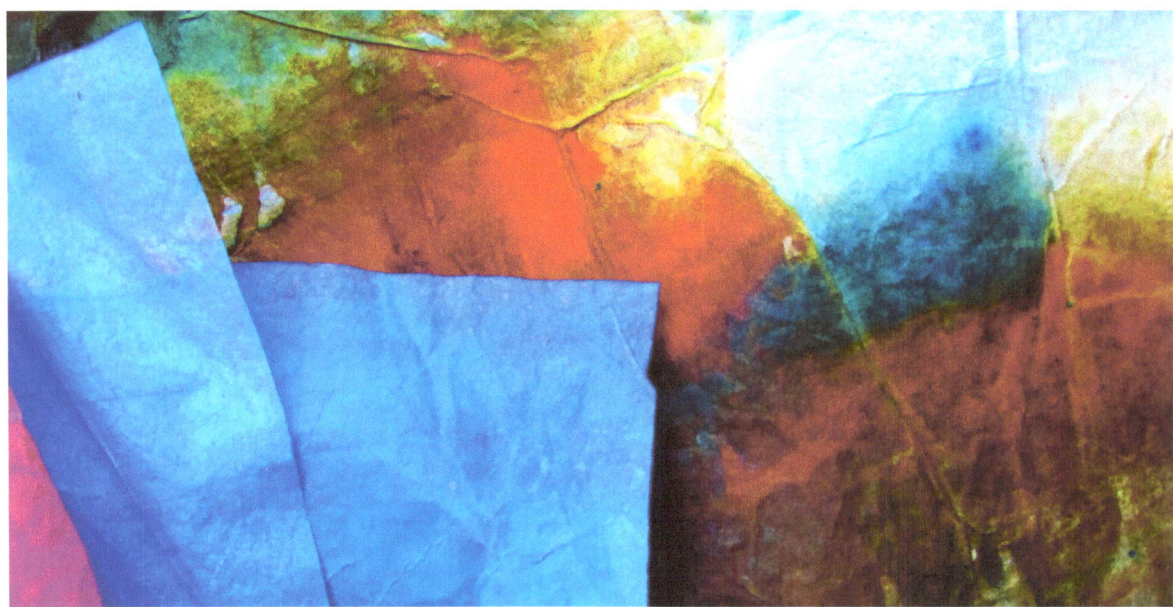

Tissue Paper covered with liquid acrylics and inks

Paper Collage and Texture
We will be looking at techniques for applying paint and/or ink to collage papers. We will stain tissue and rice paper and paint collected papers of our choice. I like to include various types of papers in my collage pieces. We'll not only discover wonderful textures in our use of tissue and rice papers, but we will also look at methods for <u>creating</u> texture (using gesso, molding/modeling pastes and various gels).

Collage is fun!

Collage in French is: "coller" which means "to glue".
Apply collage techniques to your regular style of painting, whatever your preference: landscapes, portraits, still life, geometric, florals, etc.
Make it simple... or complex.
Make a statement.
Try an abstract, textural collage with mixed media.
How about a representational collage with texture?
"Tell a story" in your collage.
Consider a "personal" collage with photos, postcards, concert tickets, buttons, etc.
Use design as the framework. Don't lose sight of basic elements and principles such as: shape, line, pattern, value, color, harmony, contrast, dominance, balance, etc.
Be artistically aware, spontaneous, intuitive, flexible and patient.
Experiment... be creative... above all, yes, have fun!

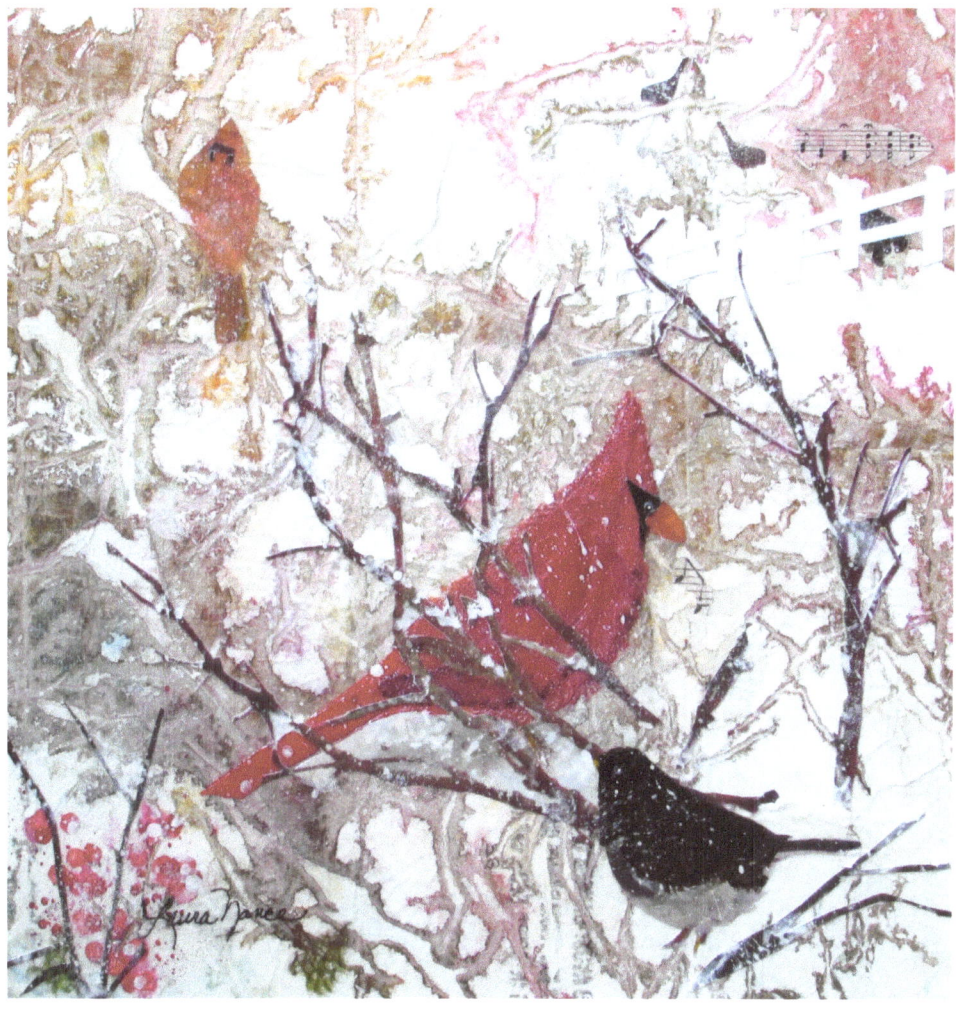

'Oh-Oh, Look Who's Coming!" Mixed Media Collage by Laura Nance

COLLAGE MATERIALS:

Tissue paper, rice paper, photos, newspapers, sheet music, poems, programs, dress patterns, maps, reproductions of art, greeting cards, ticket stubs, magazines, comic strips, packing materials, letters, corrugated paper, poster, travel brochures, stamps, wrapping paper, post cards, etc., etc.

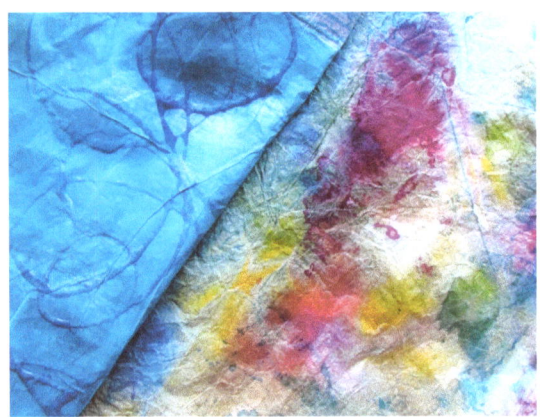

Stained / Dyed Papers

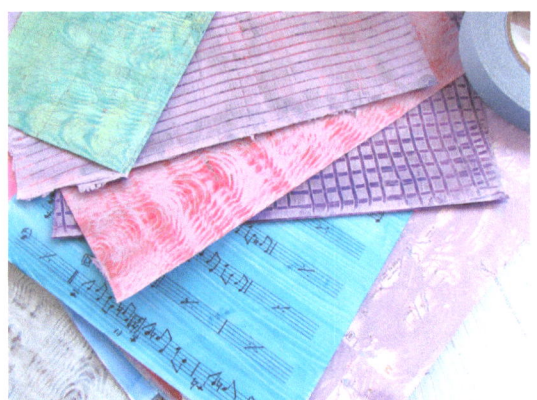

Twice Painted Personal Papers

COLLAGING BASICS:

IMPORTANT - Always make sure there is good ventilation... open windows!

When possible, use fine quality materials such as acid free papers and substrates as well as quality paints and gel mediums.

Encase supports/substrates such as matte board, or 300 lb. watercolor paper, with a medium or gel. (Apply medium or gel to front and back of support.) Use paraffin (a candle) to rub along all sides.
Take time to choose your special papers and other collaging material.

Be patient. Dry each layer of your collage before collaging on top of it.

IMPORTANT – For completed rice paper / tissue or painted papers artwork, use $\frac{3}{4}$ matte medium mixed with $\frac{1}{4}$ gloss with varnish to paint over finished artwork. Dry the work and do it again.

Wipe as much paint and gel off brushes as possible before washing them.

Collage with matte medium or a gel. Use matte medium for delicate tissue and rice paper. Use either soft gel gloss or heavy gel matte for heavier papers and objects, such as twigs and onion skin, as in the below example.

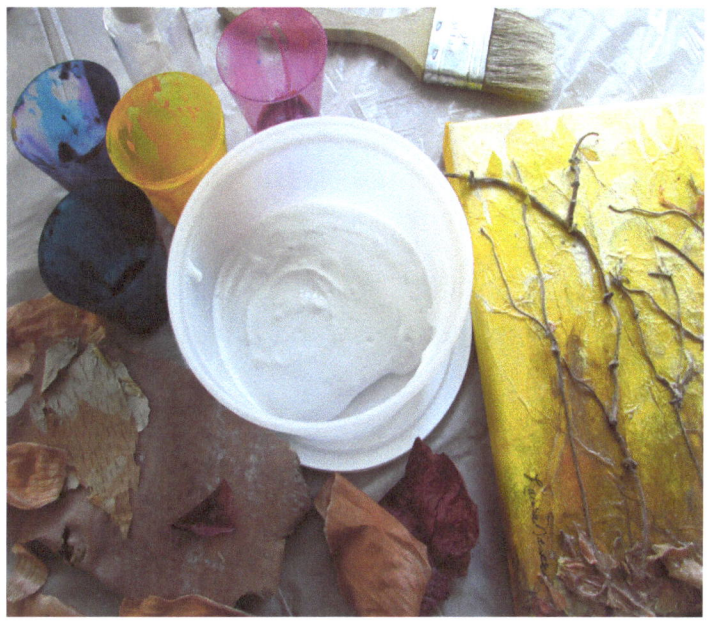

Here we find liquid acrylics and extra heavy gel matte mixed with a little water. The onion skins, tree bark, stems and twigs used for this piece have been washed and wiped with alcohol, then covered with gel. Cover the completed work with medium and varnish. Try spraying with varnish from an art supply store.

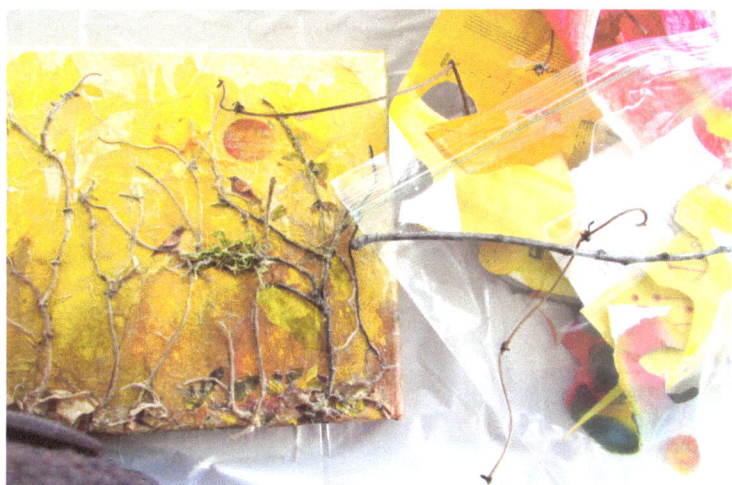

Storage: Left over papers and assorted materials used for each piece should be stored in a plastic bag for future use.
"Hazy Morn" Mixed Media Collage by Laura Nance

PREPARATION FOR COLLAGE

Supplies: Freezer paper, newspapers and tape or plastic kitchen size trash bags to fit large pieces of cardboard, several sheets of art tissue paper, rice paper, gesso, matte medium, liquid acrylic paint, acrylic ink, water filled container, several small cups or jars, eye droppers (optional), a 1" or 2" brush. Optional: a spray bottle filled with water, rubber gloves.

Important: It bears repeating... always work in a room with good ventilation... open windows when possible!

Prepare work surfaces: Each of the following two methods will work well. Either cover all working table areas with newspaper and then plastic coated freezer paper, using masking tape to secure. Or you may prefer to cover large pieces of cardboard with plastic kitchen trash bags. (Prepare several.)

Papers: Place one sheet of tissue or rice paper on top of freezer paper or a plastic trash bag.

Use fluid acrylics and water (distilled if possible). You can dilute acrylics to consistency of inks. You can dilute inks to make them less intense. (You can choose not to dilute some of the paints and inks.)
Don't use the same brush with which you're painting to mix the paint or ink with water.
You can dilute the inks or paints up to a 50/50 ratio with water.
You can mix liquid acrylics with inks. (Inks need to be shaken up.)
Mix liquid acrylic or acrylic ink with water in 3 separate jars or cups. (i.e. choose red, blue, yellow)

Think about color and composition. Always plan a color scheme, even if you don't have a specific picture in mind... 3 or 4 (one for accent). If you are new to collage, think about the colors you would like to use for your next "painting" and use some of these colors.
For the most part, we will be looking to create work that is: representational (abstract), non-objective (no imagery), abstract (cruciform or grid patterns).

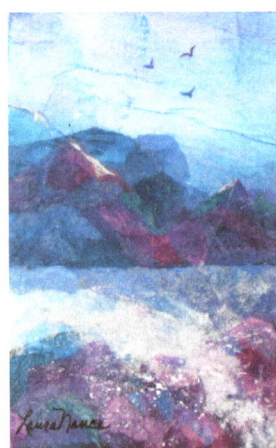

"Northern Passage"
paper collage by:
Laura Nance

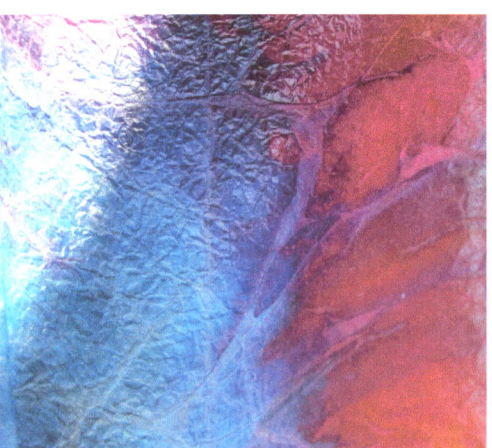

Liquid acrylic paint poured onto tissue paper... mmm... nice!

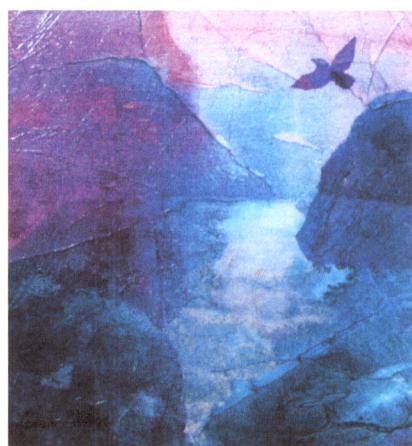

"Morning Passage"
paper collage by:
Laura Nance

STAINING TISSUES AND RICE PAPERS FOR COLLAGE

Technique: You can choose to spray the tissue or rice paper with water, or just leave it dry... either way works great. You can drop, pour or brush colors onto the papers.

Pour or drop the colors onto the tissue or rice paper.

Gently lift and tilt the covered cardboard holding the paper and watch the flow of the colors. Try to guide the paint with gentle movement to create swirls, lines, etc.

You can leave white spaces or take a damp brush and carefully blend the wet paint into those spaces (careful not to tear the paper).
Dab with paper towels when necessary.

Try laying another sheet of tissue paper on top of the wet stained paper, and, using your hand, press down. Better still, you can use a soft roller.
Carefully lift the top paper off and place it on a clean plastic trash bag. (You may need someone to help transport the wet, fragile tissue.) Doing this with a second paper might cause the first tissue to lose some of its deep or vibrant color. However, you can use either one or both of the papers for your composition.
<u>Once dried</u>, **papers can be re-stained** or painted with other colors.

Make solid color papers as well as multicolor papers... using one family of the colors of your choice.

Try painting a sheet of tissue with gesso and then let it dry. Drop liquid paint over it. When dropping paint onto paper which has been coated with gesso, colors will be brighter, with very nice texture!

Collage! Once the papers dry, we can tear, cut, draw and paint and... collage!

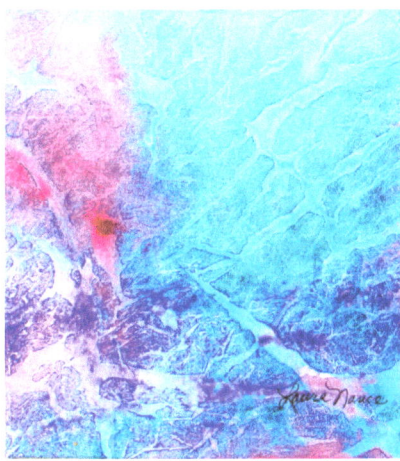

"Weathering the Storm"
by: Laura Nance

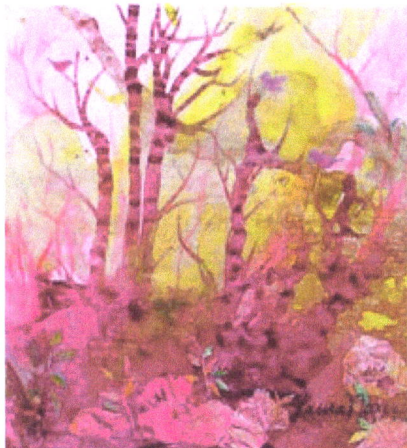

"Crimson Morn"
by: Laura Nance

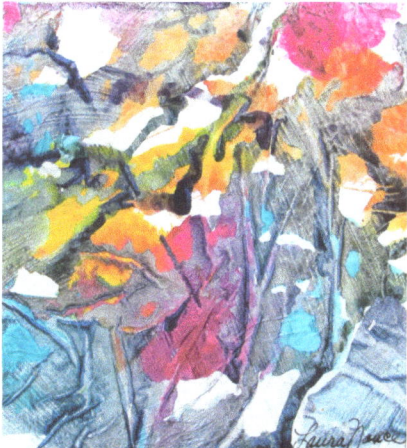

"Water's Edge"
by: Laura Nance

COLLAGING WITH TISSUES AND RICE PAPERS

Have a substrate prepared in advance.

Your ideas. Do you have a photo or picture in mind to collage?

Rescue? Have you already started a painting which needs the addition of collage to give it some pizazz?

Look carefully at your stained or painted papers.

See if there is a pattern or design you want to use as the background or even as the focal point for one of your pieces.

Artistic sense. Keep the elements of design and color in mind.

Tear or cut your papers to collage.

Be daring!

Enjoy the moment!

Paste the papers onto the prepared substrate with matte medium.

When the collage is complete, paint over it with a gloss or matte gel.

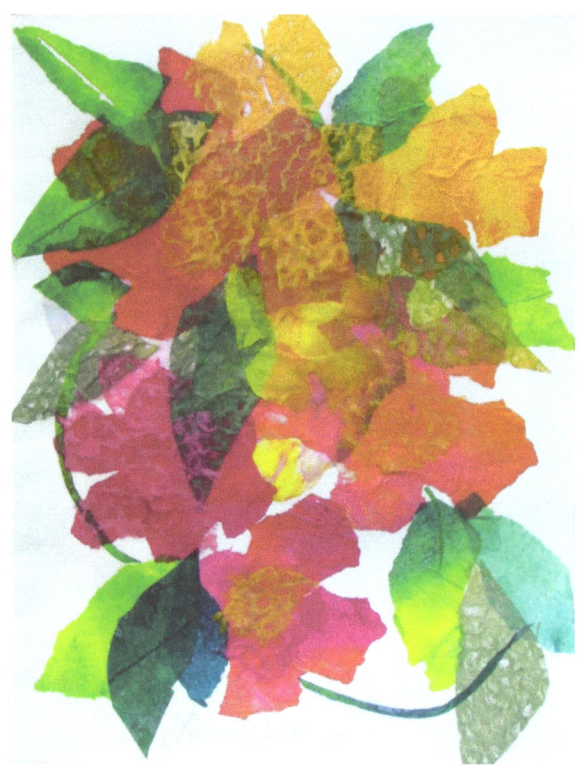

See how easy it can be?! Here is a delightful greeting card design I came up with. Just torn rice and tissue papers, glued onto prepared 300 lb. watercolor paper, with a small section of ribbon for accent!

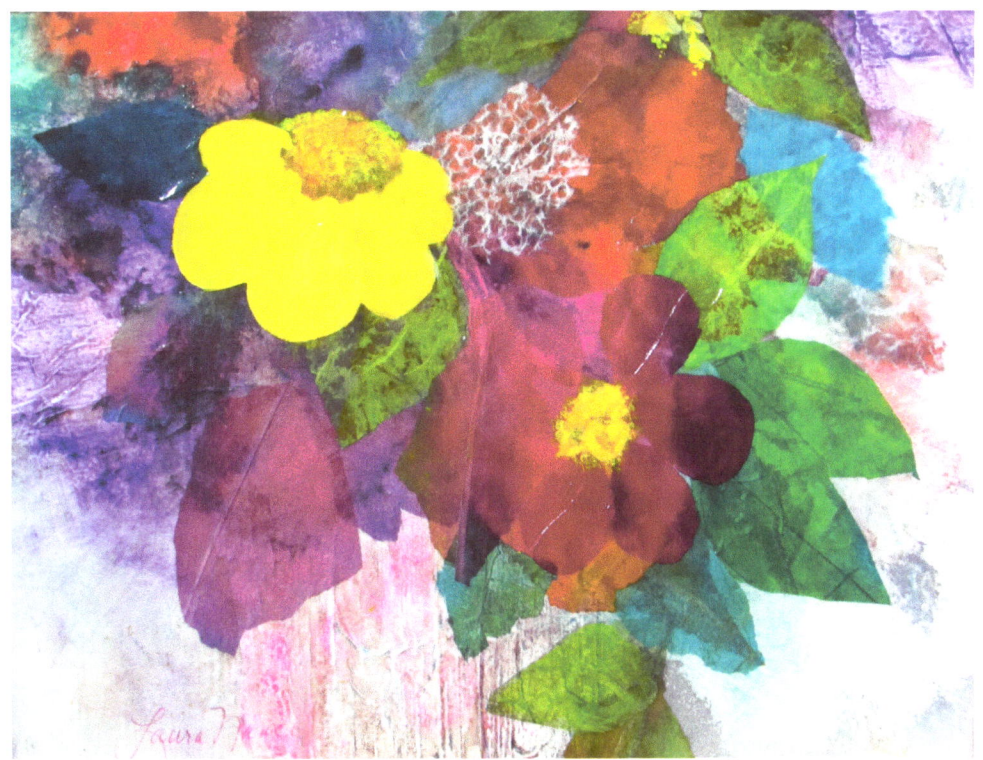

"Flowery" Assorted paper collage with added acrylic by: Laura Nance

You can see the various types of papers: some torn, others cut and shaped with scissors. The unpainted white fluff of rice paper adds flair, as does the gessoed, stained tissue paper which is the vase. I wanted more brightness and color so I painted a yellow flower and added a similar shaped magenta bloom with a yellow center.

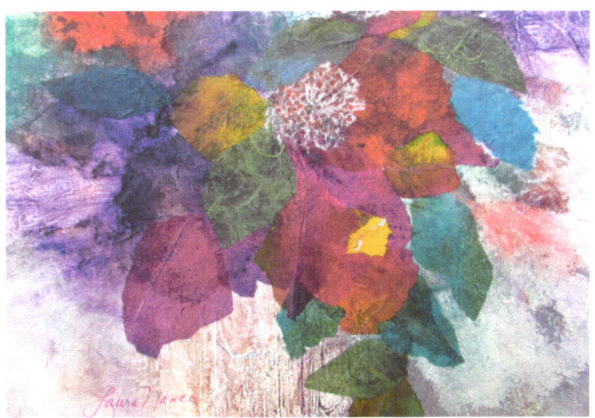

Here is the unfinished version... also lovely. We make choices as artists, and in this case... I like it either way, but I favor the finished version on top of the page.

13

PAINTING PAPERS for COLLAGE

Supplies: freezer paper and tape or plastic kitchen size trash bags to fit large pieces of cardboard, a stack of chosen papers, such as book pages, maps, pattern paper, newspaper, songs, poems, diplomas, tissue and rice paper, etc., heavy body acrylic paint, soft gel gloss or extra heavy gel matte, a water filled container, a small plastic container with a lid, a couple of 1" or 2" brushes. Optional: shaping tools, a spray bottle filled with water, rubber gloves, denatured alcohol.

Preparation: Work in a room with good ventilation... open windows...
Prepare work surfaces. Same as indicated previously. Either tape newspapers first and then freezer paper on top of working tables or cover large pieces of cardboard with plastic kitchen trash bags. (Prepare several.)
Prepare "Glue": Use either undiluted soft gel gloss, or extra heavy gel matte, diluted... about 60% to 40% water. This gel will be used as a glue to collage papers to a surface and also to coat papers previously collaged. It is best to mix gel with water ahead of time and let it sit several hours or overnight. (This will allow air bubbles to dissipate.)
Prepare Paint: Place some selected papers on top of the working area.
1st coat: Mix heavy body acrylic paint with the above mentioned gel of choice. Paint several various papers and allow them to dry.
2nd coat: Then, paint again (use the same or different color). This time, try thinning the acrylic paint with water.
While the paint is wet on the paper, you can try scraping across with different objects such as shaping tools, a wood block or even a plastic dog toy, etc.
You can spray water on the 2nd coat or blot or even experiment by dropping denatured alcohol on the wet acrylic.
If you are not satisfied with the color or design... no problem! Paint over it! The more times you paint over the paper the more interesting the texture becomes!

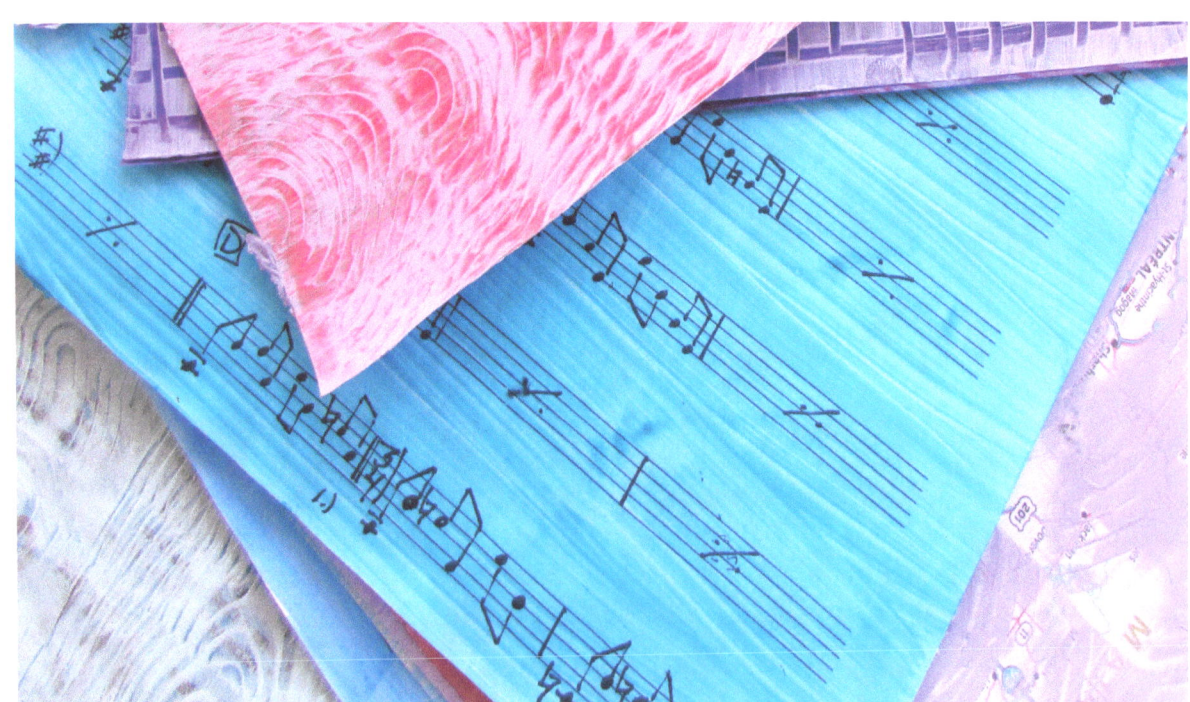

COLLAGING PAINTED PAPERS

Choose prepared substrate (canvas, illustration board, etc. covered with gesso and gel).
Paint the substrate; Use what you wish for an overall wash of color. Dry.
Cover with gel. Let it dry.
Cover substrate with painted papers. At this point, you may choose to go ahead and cover the substrate with cut strips or torn pieces of the painted / dyed papers just as a background. Do this by covering the surface with gel and then set the paper in place. You may choose to cover the back of any thicker quality paper with gel, as well. Press down to make sure it is set in place (be careful, as some of the delicate papers tear easily).
Choose an image you would like to collage.
Cut this image out.
This could be a drawing, photographed object or subject which you would like to recreate.
Prepare to cut three or more copies of the subject.
Choose papers... several painted or stained papers – all of which you will tape together.
Tape the painted or stained papers together with the pre-cut subject you wish to recreate for your collage. Place the detailed piece on top (I sometimes like to place tracing paper on the very top and pencil out details). Having taped all papers together...
Cut out your copies!
You can draw details later. The paper can be painted over if need be.
Once the images are cut, you can begin to collage.
Cover the substrate with the gel.
Carefully cover the back of one of the papers you have cut with gel and set it in place on your canvas / surface. Press into place with your hand or use a roller for larger pieces.
Brush gel over the glued papers. (For small pieces, I sometimes use my fingers instead of a brush... you can wear gloves, or not).
Repeat the procedure with other items you plan on using for the piece, until collage is complete, attaching cut papers and covering with gel. The more gel the better!
You can think about using textures like straw or fabric, etc. as in "Sweet Hands" collage.

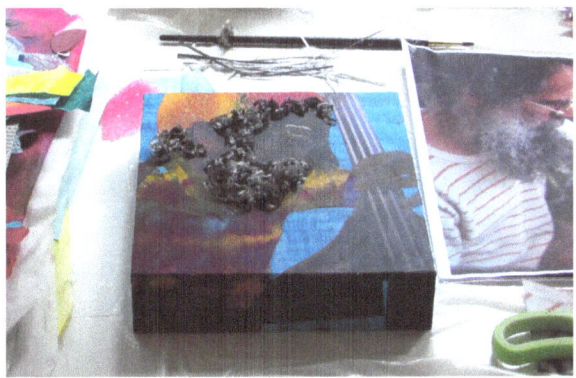

A glimpse into Laura's studio. You can see the above work in progress... a paintbrush with thin strips of paper wrapped around it for "hair"... the original image for "Ethiopian Blues" is my husband, Robert... who is also a great bass player!

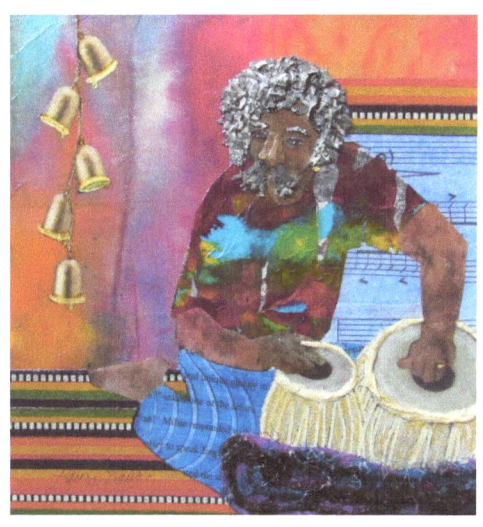

"Sweet Hands"
Mixed Media Collage by:
Laura Nance

CREATING SKINS - Marbled or Solid

Note: Any gel or even just plain acrylic paint will create a gel skin!

Tape or secure a plastic sheet protector onto an illustration board or on top of a trash bag covered cardboard.

Pour out Matte Medium (you can also add a pouring medium on top of it for a lighter consistency) – spread with a palette knife.

Drop (small dots of) color (liquid acrylics or heavy body thinned with a medium) onto wet medium – using applicator bottles. Use colors you like – Look for contrast - Colors which will work well together – i.e. blue ultramarine, cobalt teal, turquoise phalo, violet.

Create a pattern - Take a sharp pointy tool i.e. clay sculpting tools, wood carving tools, palette knives, forks, nails, toothpicks... etc and move the paint around... try "scrolling" or "swirling" movements, etc.

If desired, you can do a definite pattern.

When dry, lift off the gel and use or store between sheets of waxed paper.

If not using right away, you can coat the gel skin with matte medium or clear gesso to keep it from sticking to other surfaces.

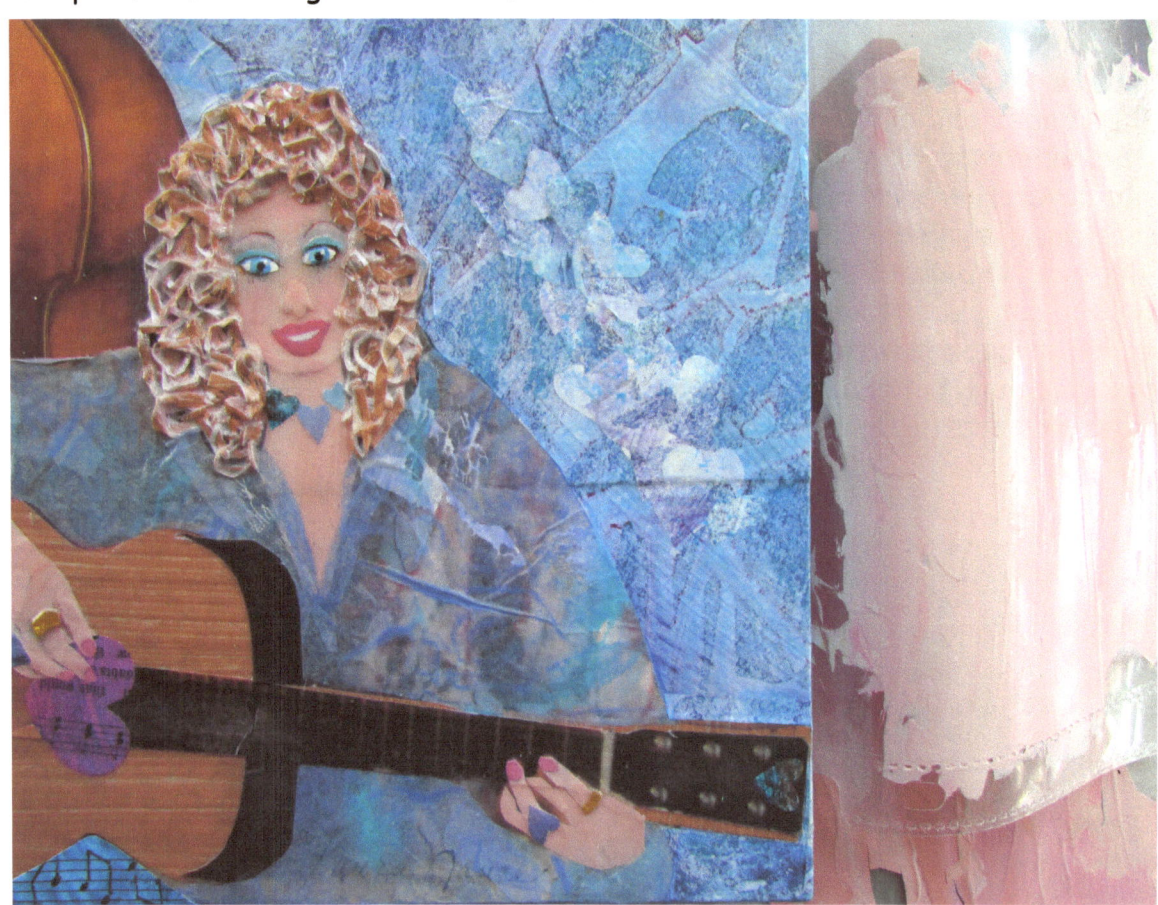

"Double Bass With Six Strings" by Laura Nance   Acrylic "Skin"

Note: I created various tones of pink and brown gel skins which I used as skin for characters in some of my collages. Here you see a cropped portion of my work "Double Bass With Six Strings" on the left and an example of the skin tones created on the plastic sheet protector to the right. As you can see, the acrylic skin was used for the face and hands in this piece.

MANIPULATING / MOLDING TISSUE PAPER

Here is an example of how you can mold and shape tissue paper. For this piece, I created a large tree in the foreground by manipulating tissue paper with heavy gel. You can work with it on the plastic kitchen bag as I did, or on the treated side of freezer paper. I allowed the newly formed trunk and branches to dry and then used the heavy gel mixed with some water to apply the pieces to my canvas. The finished piece also has a fence cut out of heavy watercolor paper and additional trees created by using molding paste with gel.

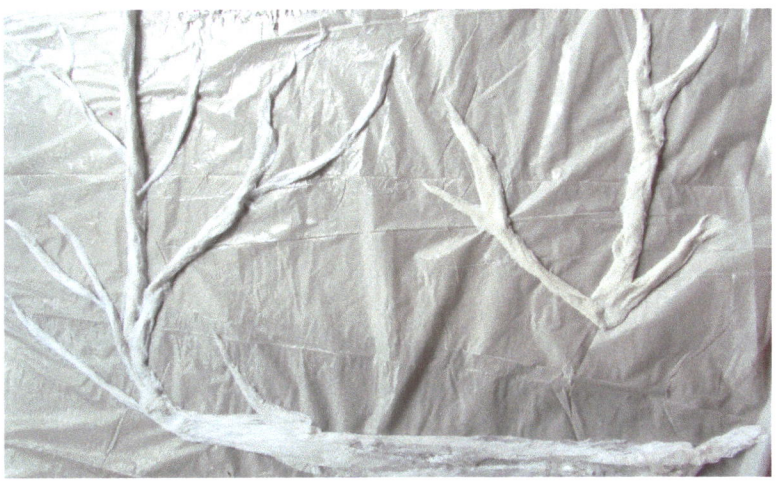

Tissue paper manipulated with heavy gel matte and water.

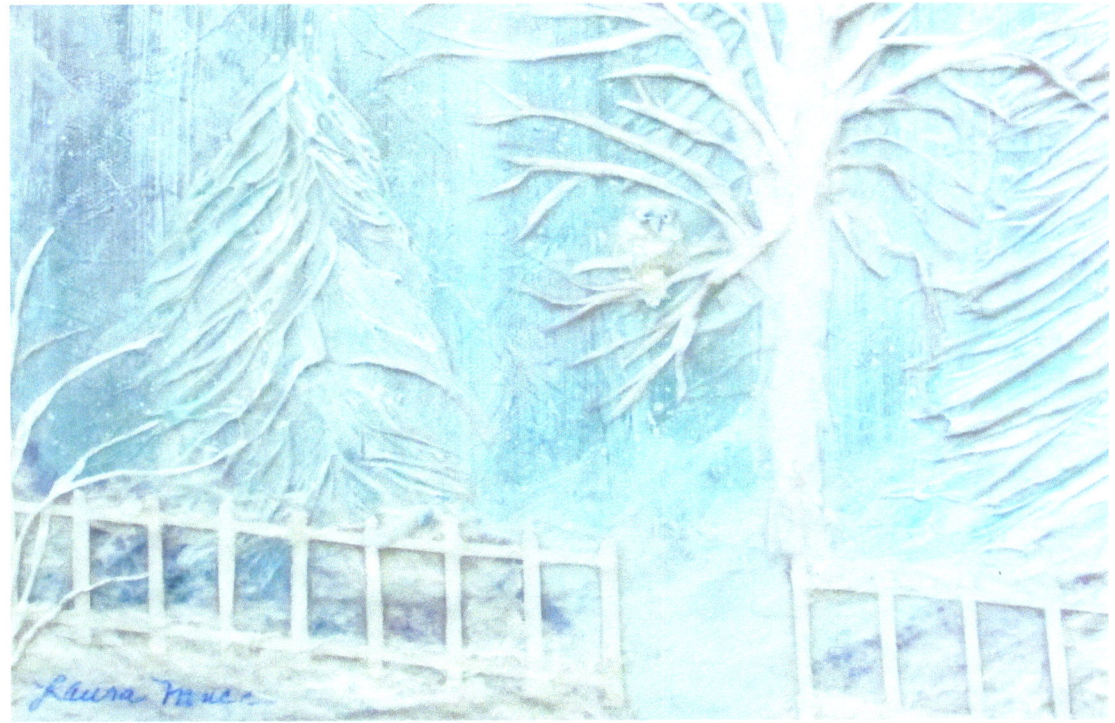

This is a clipped version of my work, "Out In The Cold" where you can see not only the tree but an owl which was also created out of tissue paper.

PULL-APART TEXTURAL TECHNIQUE

This is such a simple, but fun technique which can really produce interesting results.
Apply a generous amount of gel, heavy body acrylic paint or a combination of paint and
a medium onto a (prepared) small canvas, illustration board, or heavy watercolor paper.
Place a second canvas or paper on top of wet gel/paint.
Press together... then quickly pull pieces apart.
Observe the neat branch-like crevices or patterns.
Let these images dry thoroughly.
You can paint and collage around the image.

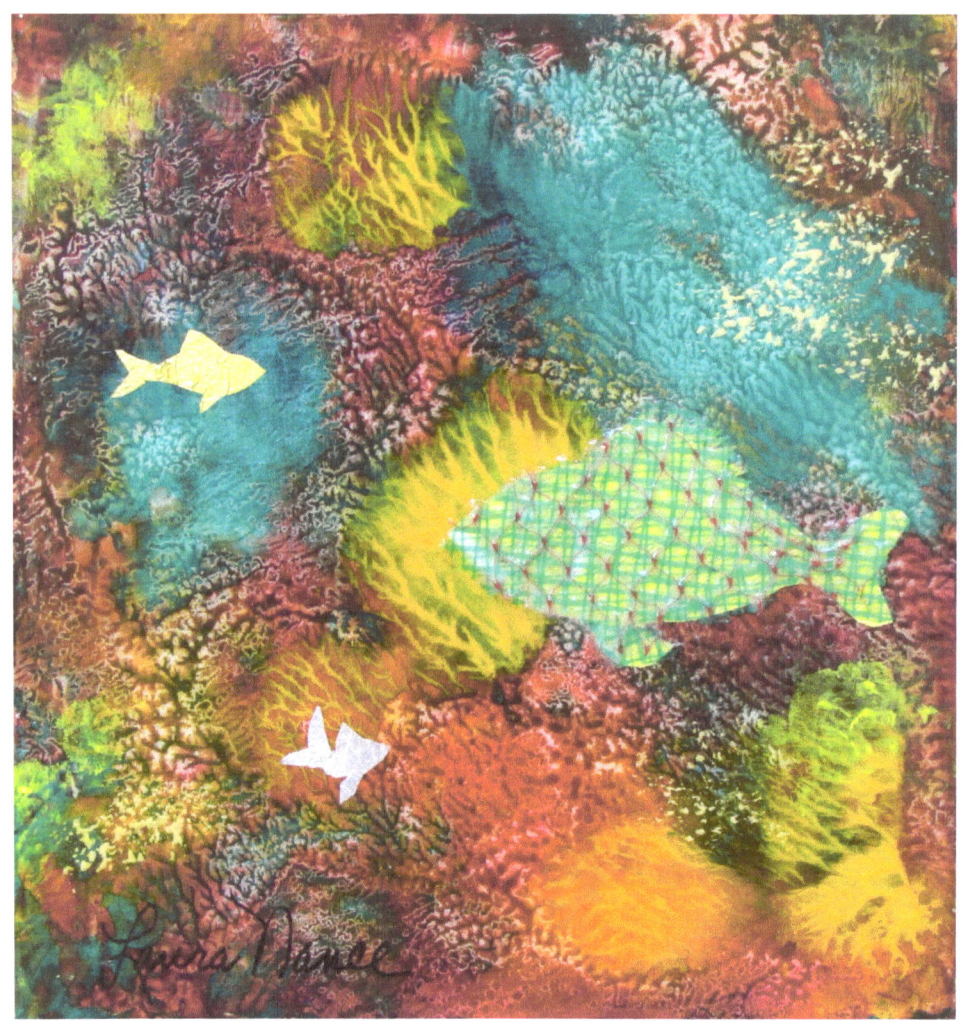

"Jacque's World" Mixed Media Acrylic/Collage by Laura Nance
Here you can see several examples of the results of the pull-apart
technique, particularly in the yellow sea life. You can also see how "produce bags" were useful for texturing a fish. The silver and gold colored
fish were shaped from candy wrappers.

MIXED MEDIA - COLLAGE WITH TEXTURE

I started this piece by priming a wooden substrate with gesso. Then, a palette knife was used to shape a mixture of molding paste and gel into a vase and five blooms. I allowed that to dry for a couple of days. Mixing acrylic paint with water, I painted (and to achieve a softer appearance, blotted with paper towels) the blooms and vase. Contrary to ordinary procedure, after allowing the paint to dry, I then added the background colors with paint and collage (including a small scrap of printed material just for fun). For special effect, and to heighten the organic feel of the piece, I added "vines" of raffia.

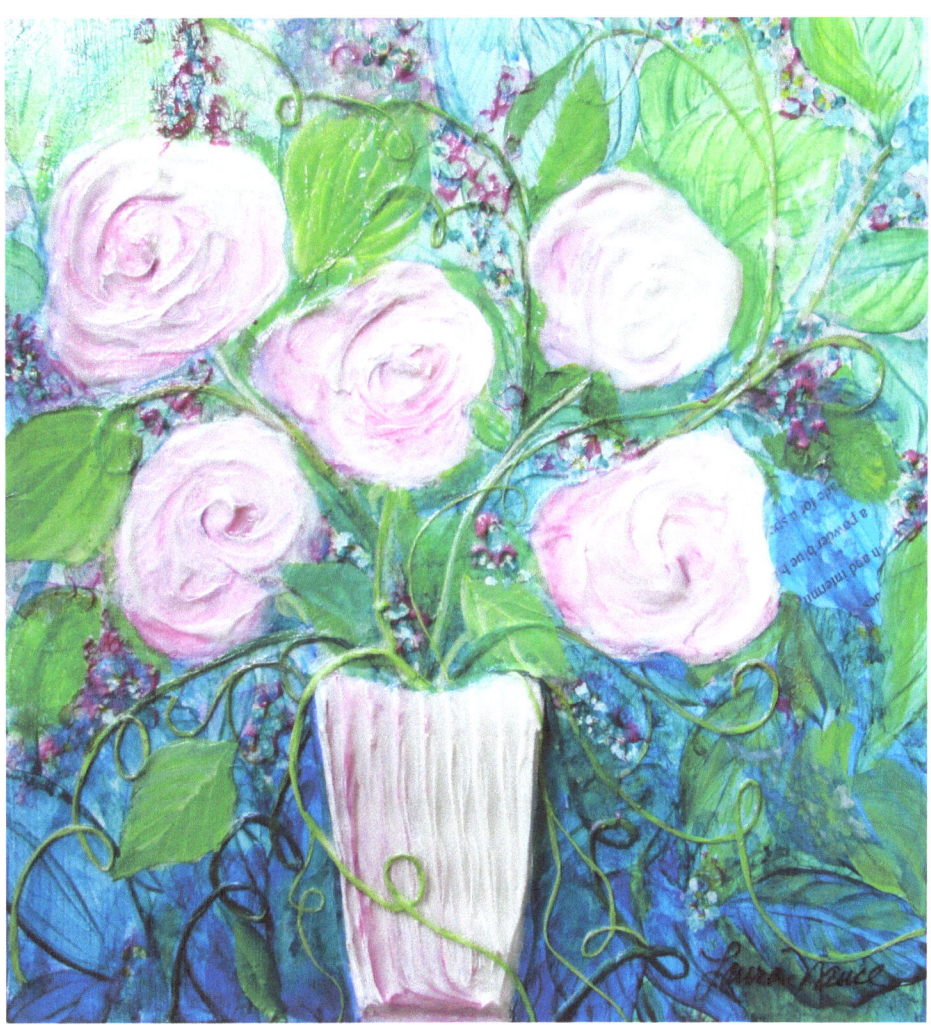

"Sherbet Flowers" Mixed Media by Laura Nance

IMAGE TRANSFERS - Day One

Choose an image.
Use an image that is printed from a laser printer (not an inkjet).
Your image can come from a photograph, a magazine or catalog. I like using copies of my artwork as transfers.
Have the image printed onto cheaper quality paper. This seems to work best in the transfer process.
Remember, your final image, after the transfer, will be "reversed".

Note: You may want to have two or three copies of the image printed if you plan on collaging any portion of the image after it's been transferred.
You can transfer on top of an otherwise completed and dried acrylic painting.
Transfers should be made on a prepared (gesso) sturdy surface.
Paint the substrate with a light colored acrylic. Dry.
Using a dry brush... Apply gel medium to the surface. Let it Dry.

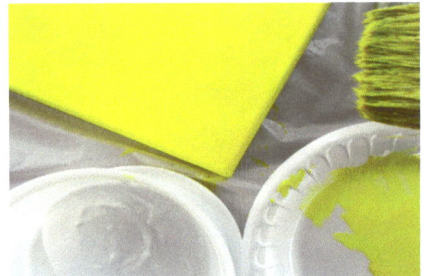

Paint prepared surface.

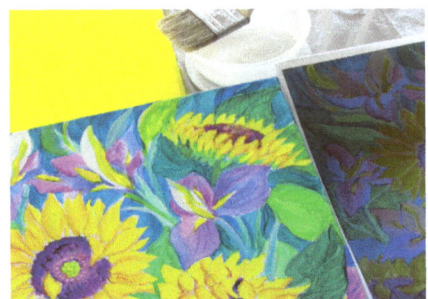

Apply gel medium over dried paint. See original painting along with laser image.

Apply gel medium again, (one section at a time for larger pieces)... lay the laser image <u>face down</u> **on the wet gel, moving quickly.**
Leave enough paper to fall over the edges of the substrate.
Press down – and flatten the image with your hands - if possible, use a roller.
Note: Don't get gel medium on top of the paper being transferred.
Let it dry overnight.

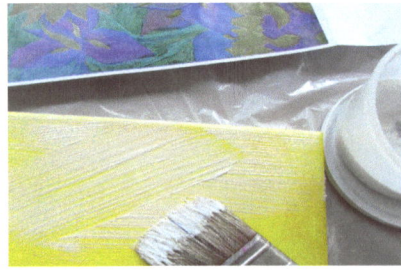

Apply the gel medium again.

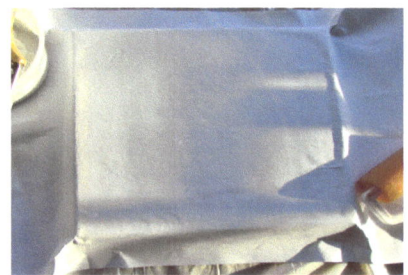

Work carefully and quickly, lay laser image face down on the wet gel surface, using a roller to flatten and secure. Let dry overnight.

IMAGE TRANSFERS - Day Two

Next day... remove the top paper layer from your canvas:

Spray with water or dampen with a wet sponge. Give it a few minutes to allow the water to soak in.
Begin rubbing carefully. You can peel/rub with your fingers – or try using a dry sponge. I have discovered the best way is by using a combination sponge/scrubber – purchased from your local supermarket.

Once your transferred image is dry... proceed with creating/developing the rest of the piece!

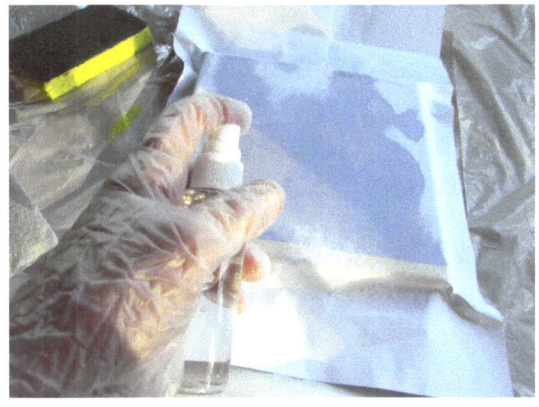

Spray dried laser image with water.

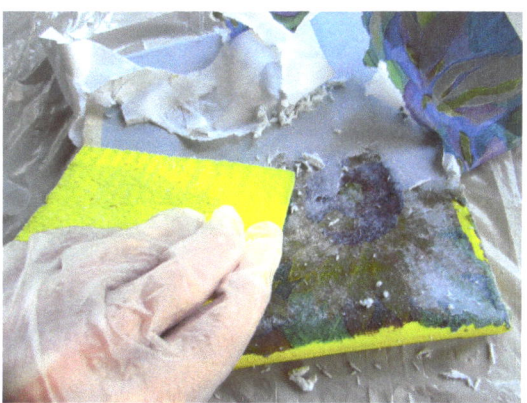

Rub carefully using sponge/scrubber.

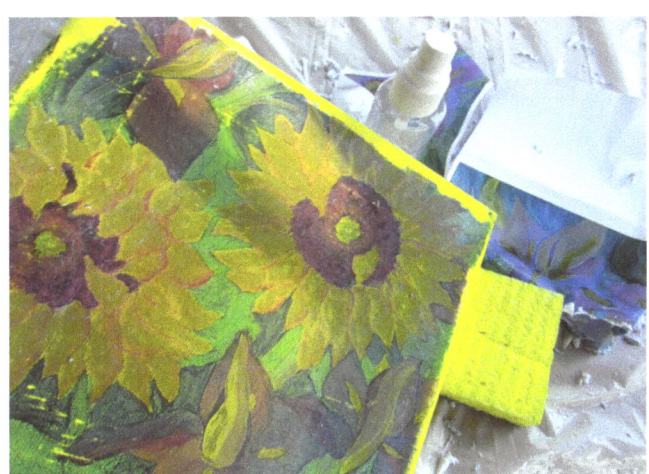

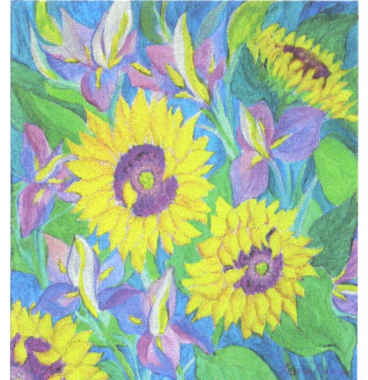

"Invitation" original acrylic by:
Laura Nance

Here is the transfer, moments following first paper removal. It is still wet and has a fine paper film remaining. Let it dry and then, with a lightly dampened sponge, rub off any remaining paper. Once dry, let the transfer inspire you to collage and paint your masterpiece. Any space where the transfer does not take, will give the piece a nice antique effect allowing the under paint to show.

RESCUING ABANDONED WORK

Do you have "abandoned artwork"? Have you ever labored diligently over a work which never came together? A piece which you finally abandoned?

Try collage!

I re-discovered such a sorry canvas in a storage closet. It's painted side was facing the wall, just as I had placed it years before. I brought it into my studio where I dropped acrylic paint over portions of the work, leaving some of the original background colors there. I suddenly got excited over the idea of adding collage to the piece. As I looked at the canvas, the magenta tones reminded me of bougainvilleas, and how I had first discovered the blooms while on a cruise to the Bahamas, many years ago.

I tore and cut stained tissue in various tones of magenta, pink, apricot and yellow. Then, I covered each little petal with gel, prior to attaching it to the substrate. Working quickly, I decided to include a couple of birds in the scene, as well as a touch of straw for nesting material. I cut vines and leaves out of painted papers, and for additional texture, added some leaves made of cheesecloth.

It was great fun to see how the "rescued" work developed... moment by moment... into an interesting piece!

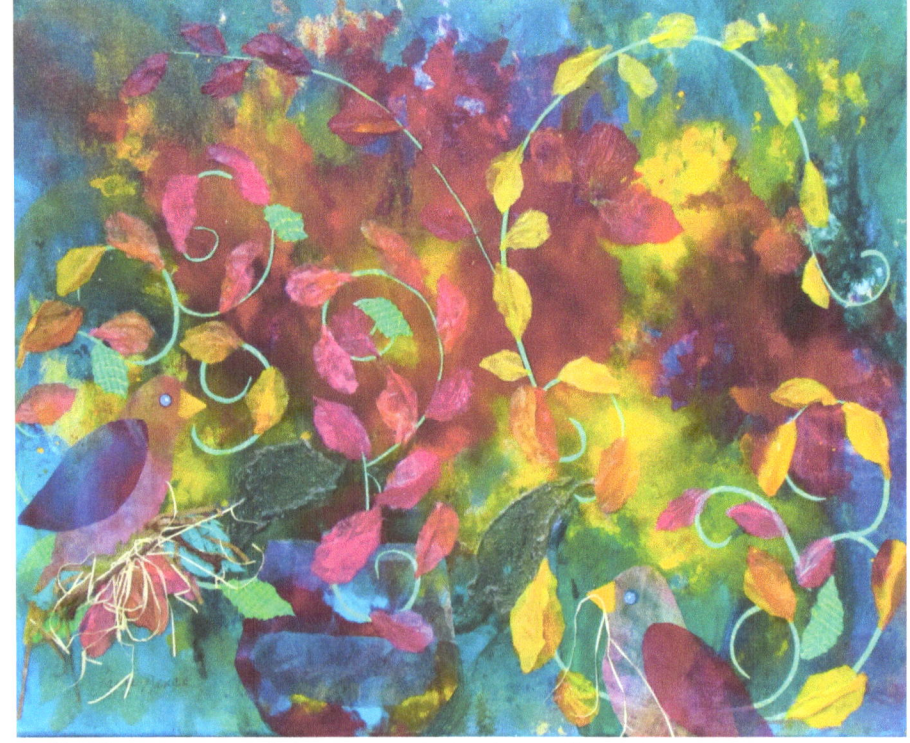

"Villa Bougainvillea" Mixed Media Collage by Laura Nance

I hope you enjoyed and were inspired as you read through the pages of this book. Most of all, may you feel encouraged to incorporate these workshop techniques in creating your own art.

Please let others know about this book and that copies can be obtained directly from: Amazon.com

Thanks so much!
Laura

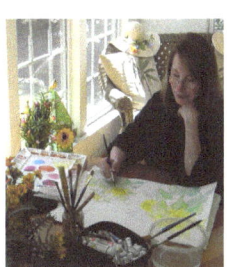

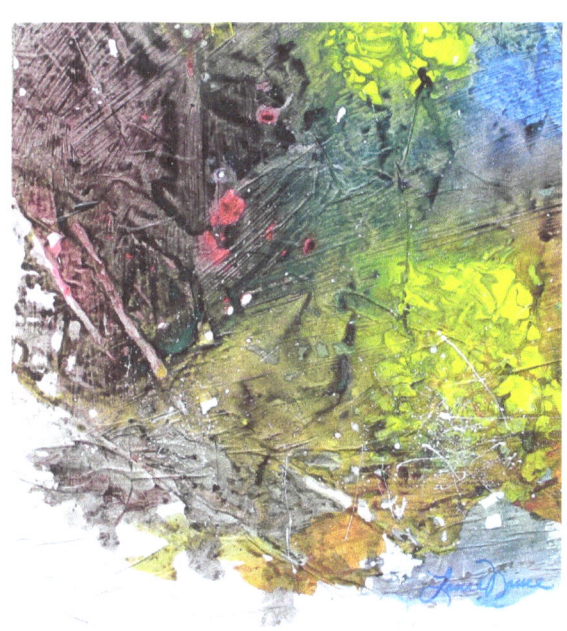

"Secluded" watermedia, paper collage by: Laura Nance

For purchase of Laura's artwork or for information regarding Workshops or Private Classes with Laura, send all inquiries by email to: allthingsconsist@aol.com
Visit Laura's website:
http://laura-nance.fineartamerica.com

Copies of this book can be purchased at: Amazon.com

NOTES:

NOTES:

www.ingramcontent.com/pod-product-compliance
Lightning Source LLC
Chambersburg PA
CBHW050434180526
45159CB00006B/2534